What in the World is Going On?

A self help book that reveals the criteria of happiness derived from knowing the facts of morality

Prick

Bloomington, IN 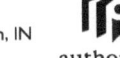 Milton Keynes, UK

authorHOUSE®

AuthorHouse™
1663 Liberty Drive, Suite 200
Bloomington, IN 47403
www.authorhouse.com
Phone: 1-800-839-8640

AuthorHouse™ UK Ltd.
500 Avebury Boulevard
Central Milton Keynes, MK9 2BE
www.authorhouse.co.uk
Phone: 08001974150

First published by AuthorHouse 12/19/2006

ISBN: 978-1-4259-7680-4 (sc)

Printed in the United States of America
Bloomington, Indiana

This book is printed on acid-free paper.

Dedicated to the Creator of all life

CONTENTS

INTRODUCTION

Throughout my adult life I searched and searched for the knowledge that would give me the facts of life and how to live it. I found those facts scattered in psychology, new age, and philosophy. I never found them all under one author. So I decided to write it myself.

My first book, 'The Truth Nobody Told You' was my first attempt at identifying the most important areas of life and how to deal with them. I finished that book in August of 2005, but my knowledge kept growing and now here it is October of 2006 and this second book is now complete. Both books cover the same areas, in general but there are some details that are in one and not the other. Nothing in my first book is contradicted in my second one; those ideas I put forth in the first one are still held as true in the second one. The main difference with my second book is it is written from a more mature viewpoint than the first one—my knowledge is more in-depth and complete.

What could you expect to gain from reading these books? You could gain a new theory of good and evil rooted firmly in the facts of reality; you could gain a path to bring you from the shadows of doubt into the light of certainty. No longer would you look at yourself and others as an 'unknown quantity'.

As in the first book my structure is more free flowing than constrained and I bring up the same points again and again throughout the book. For example, chapter three and chapter five cover 'similar ground'. My progression of thought and experimentation on myself led my understanding to add chapter five as new insights came available to me. Look at the book as a collection of ideas talking about only three major subjects: life with yourself; life with others; and the basic nature of good and evil.

I intend this book to be a self help book, in that it can tell you your basic nature and how to achieve your happiness. It can tell you the basic nature of society and it can tell you how to get ready for the new age of Aquarius. In a word it gives the knowledge that can enable you to be all you can be. What you will do with this knowledge, if anything, is up to you!

CHAPTER ONE
Who you are and where you are

1. Where you are

The general nature of reality is that it is GOOD—it is BENEVOLENT. I do not care what experience you are involved in on earth it still remains true that it is taking place in a benevolent universe. If you think about this you must necessarily come to the same conclusion that this is so because, can you imagine that for the universe to be bad or malevolent and life to be nothing but a pain factory there would be no point in living? I mean who would want this?

The next obvious question, then, is what explains all the horrible realities that many people are experiencing on earth? **Really, the root cause of most of the pain and suffering that exists on earth is because the philosophy that is predominant the world over is** '**power-trip tribalism**'. This tribalism philosophy is the false philosophy because it goes against human nature. Man is not meant to be a tribal member or leader, he is meant to be a soveirgn, independent, reasoning, free feeling being that has the right to live for his own benefit—that is how he is made. This true philosophy of independence/free will is the right one for mankind and sanctions thinking and feeling. Tribalism is the false philosophy and is against the feelings and the moral truth.

Within the tribalist philosophy each individual is regarded as part of the tribe with no moral significance other than to serve his brother and the tribe. He is taught that his relationship with others (the tribe) is 'all' and his relationship with himself is nothing. He must therefore gain his happiness from the impossible criteria of self sacrifice for his brother. Listen to most of the religions and so called philosophies of the world which promote tribalism and you can hear them openly express this morality of self sacrifice/tribalism as the highest good.... But, what is the bottom line of tribalism and why does it have such dominance in the world?

Tribalism in essence is a 'mentalism' philosophy; its major characteristics are: thinking, but not in the truth of morality since that would show tribalism to be false; and, keeping the feelings denied. This philosophy appeals to most people mainly because it keeps the feelings denied.

Because the tribalists deny their feelings, they are wrong. Consequently, they sense that anyone living in the truth of thinking and feeling by holding independence as the true philosophy poses a threat to their false philosophy and is seen as an enemy to be defeated.

This is where the use of their power trips comes in. These trips come in four forms: order trips, guilt trips, fear trips and hate trips. They use these trips on the free will state people get into and these trips purpose is to hurt the will/feelings. It is by this means they hope you will give up your feelings like they have done and concede that tribalism is right. Again, the major reason they accept tribalism is because it denies the feelings and it is the feelings that the tribalist does not want to live with and, **he doesn't want you to live with your feelings either.**

Repeating this very important truth about these two philosophies is to say that, generally speaking, tribalism promotes a 'mental only' state of being and requires the will/feelings to be denied. With the free will philosophy (the true one) both 'thinking and feeling' are sanctioned. The beauty of knowing this discrimination is that you can remember that these two states are the only two major states that play out with people and is the simplest way to categorize them, i.e. identify them. But, what is it about the feelings the tribalist doesn't want to accept?

Inside each of us, at the feeling level, are 3 pools—of fear, rage and grief. God calls this 'lost will' because it's held down in the subconscious and kept in denial by each of us. You must also know that the type of evolution we are engaged in is from that of denying the will (feelings), to that of evolving into accepting the will. Ethically, this means that we need to evolve from tribalism to embracing free will/independence. So really, tribalism, which effectively shuts the will down is an evolutionary thing, and since we denied the will because we didn't know any other way to deal with lost will, tribalism 'solved' the problem by denying the entire will. The down side of tribalism is that it engenders falsehoods and also eliminates free will. Consequently, the adherent could never achieve happiness through following the tenets of tribalism because it goes against the truth of human nature. However, it does eliminate him having to deal with his feelings which is the biggest undertaking in evolution.

Well, so what is the solution? **In a simple statement, the solution is to quit initiating power tripping others; feel your emotions and quit denying them; bring your thinking up to learn that independence/free will is the moral truth and tribalism is false; and finally learn how to deal the tribalist.**

By you stopping yourself initiating power tripping others, you will stop earning true guilt. By you beginning to accept your feelings, primarily the fear, rage and grief and allowing them to express, a little at a time, is exactly what is going to heal them. By you accepting reason's truth including the morality of independence, your mind will work better than ever because you won't be holding the contradictions of tribalism any longer. By you dealing with the tribalists in an effective manner you will stop them from preventing you to practice this truth of freedom—namely you living with your will 'online' and in joy. I want only to show you, here in this chapter the problem and solution. To implement the solution is going to be the biggest job you will ever have to do so for now just consider this with your understanding.

So that's the general nature of the **important conditions** man faces (where you are) but what is the essentials of mans nature (who you are)?

*   *   *

2. Who you are

Humans are Gods and Goddesses! We are offspring of God are we not? Yes, so, we are Gods and Goddesses ourselves—a simple, logical deduction. The identification of being, then, either God or each of us, is the same thing...... Fine, so what is that nature?

In the simplest terms we are a fivefold being. We **think**, we **feel**, we **love** and we **see**. Finally, we **orchestrate** these previous four energies. These are the five energies that make each of us up. They are called: 1.spirit/mind energy, 2.will/feelings energy, 3.heart/love energy, 4.body/sight energy, and 5.the Orchestrator energy of these previous four, the conscious/subconscious energy (c/sc). All five energies have one main job each.

For the spirit/mind energy, its job is to deal with identifying and evaluating reality, in conceptual terms—in words. This power is called 'reason'. It can tell you what things are and also their value. This power deals in thoughts.

The next energy is the will/emotion energy. This energy expresses emotion to tell you what your values are and also if your values are being achieved or frustrated. They will express exactly what your 'value structure' holds as right and wrong, as valuable and not valuable, as for you or against you. So, as you go through your day you will feel emotions in response to your experiences and they will always be a reflection of your value structure. Your will is constantly evaluating yourself and the reality facing you with reference to your value structure and will give you a running tally on how you are doing moment by moment. If you are interested in understanding your will/feeling energy you must understand the values in your value structure because these are exactly what your emotions express.

All emotions are 'value' oriented in nature. Look at any emotion the feelings express and you can see its tie to value. Fear, for example, is an emotion that tells you one or more of your values are threatened. Rage is a feeling of value frustration. Envy is usually because another has a value you do not have. The feeling of true guilt is because you have violated one of your values—your 'right and wrong (value) structure'. Grief is usually the response of losing a value, e.g. a loved one dies (whom you valued). Hate is a response to someone who try's to stop you pursuing your values or threatens you for having them. Pain tells you you are pursuing a wrong value, e.g. touching a hot stove or holding the ethics of tribalism. Joy is the response to value fulfillment or attainment, (and is worth all the tea in china!). These value oriented emotions are what the feeling body expresses, and they will faithfully follow your value structure.

All of the emotions you feel can be identified in words which will explain exactly why you are feeling any given emotion. If, as an example, you are crossing the street and a car comes barreling down on you, after you recognize the danger, your emotions will emote fear to tell you your life is threatened. In this instance you know exactly why you feel the emotion. It is the same with any other emotion. So, if you are experiencing emotional upset and you don't know why, you can look into your value structure to find the values involved that create the emotion. Through examining your values you can learn to resolve upset emotions, i.e. heal the value conflict and the emotions will smooth out as a result.

They (the emotions), will always express your value structure no matter what your value structure contains. If you hold false values your emotions will still emote according to your values as if they were true. It is because of this that a thief, for example, will feel elation if he comes across, say, a car with the keys in it—he values stealing things and when he sees an opportunity to do so, his emotions will emote joy in accordance to his (false) values.

The heart energy is the third part of being, hierarchically. Its job is to deal with acceptance and rejection. Another word for love is acceptance and what the heart has to accept is all five parts of being and the entirety of creation. Since spirit and will balances in the heart, non-denial of these first two energies, by the being, is good for the heart as well as the spirit and the will. Realizing that the denial of the will in evolution by each of us created a massive imbalance between mind and will, the heart didn't have a chance to live. Accepting the will will enable this third power to exist and 'come into its own'. Unconditional love is the goal of the heart.

The body energy is responsible for creating form and gaining information of a visual type—picture knowledge.

It is with the use of sight that body can create form. The power of this level I call 'Beauty' because true form of which the body creates is always beautiful—this is power number four. When your eyes are seeing the beauty of your surroundings this energy is in it's 'up state'.

The fifth energy is the conscious/subconscious, c/sc. The role of it is to be the orchestrator of the previous four energies in a balanced and harmonious way. In conclusion, then, the being can be likened to a four piece orchestra **and** a conductor.

Reason, Freedom, Love, Beauty, and Harmony are the names I use to refer to these five wonderful, cosmic powers of these five parts of being. If you would work on developing these powers you will be investing in forever and preparing yourself for the Age of Aquarius of which we are on the doorstep. Actually there is nothing more valuable for you to do than to understand yourself and it is much easier to do this work than it is to stay in ignorance and lead a 'normal' life. If you were to realize that our sojourn into tribalism is finished (which, at its worst, included misery, murder, rape and pillage,) and that now evolution simply becomes recognizing and developing the glorious powers of free will, reason, love, beauty and harmony the question boils down to, do you have acceptance for all these good things in life, and are you willing to accept all of your feelings? On accepting your feelings much needs to be said and I will cover this later.

The net of tribalism will rise up against you when you take this road toward self fulfillment and I hope to show you how to deal with this later in this book.

*   *   *

Summary of the essentials

What I have explained about the general nature of reality (where you are) and the nature of being (who you are) needs to be summarized for you to better able retain it.

So, I started by saying reality is benevolent but that we are under the influence of the traditional false philosophy of tribalism and that this is why things are so screwed up on earth—'nobody gets their own space' under this system. Remember that this age old experience in tribalism was necessary for man's understanding in order to learn exactly why we need reason and free will by trying to live without them. **That time is over.** It is now time that we should begin to live in free will and the moral truth of individual rights. In order to do this we must know the truth of good and evil completely and this is exactly the knowledge I give in this book.

Next, I described the purpose of tribalism as being against the will/feelings because no one knew how to deal with lost will. Specifically, lost will contains fear/ terror, anger/rage and sadness/grief and in order to short circuit these feelings, tribalism was adopted as the true morality. So, you can know that the tribalist is a mental only person—he has his feelings in denial. What's more, the tribalist is against anyone practicing free will because it represents a threat to his false morality. If he were to accept free will he would have to 'feel' and this is exactly the thing he does not want to do.

I then said the solution to this state of affairs is threefold: 1 quit **initiating** power tripping others, 2. start accepting your feelings, 3 learn the true morality of 'stand on your own two feet' independence, i.e. ditch tribalism and pick up free will and truth! (I will be talking just how to live standing on your own later in this book.)

I would like to add that all the manifestations of anti-individualism throughout the past, such as communism or socialism, were upheld by the people because it short circuited the feelings. You can notice that since the few free will proponents in the past didn't know the ethics of independence this allowed the ethics of tribalism to stand unchallenged and say that self sacrifice i.e. tribalism, was the truth. Little did anyone know then, that the reason for the tribalist ethics was to kill the feelings of the will because another way to deal with the fear, rage and grief inside all of us, wasn't known.

In today's times this tribalist philosophy persists intact and governs the entire 'net of tribalism' which most people subscribe to, at least in part. The form it takes is when a person exercises free will/independence he is assaulted with orders, guilt trips, fear trips and hate trips by other members of the tribe and the purpose of these 'trips' is to make him give up reason, independence ethics, **and his feelings.** Even though tribalism provided a means to get along with others without rocking the boat (of anti independence), it went against human nature. This then resulted in pain and misery of the members of which they had to deny or lie to themselves about in order to continue to believe the tribe orientation was right. Therefore, the choice became: 1. become a tribalist and get along with others but deny the guilt of holding the death ethics since this is what is socially acceptable or 2. Uphold the true ethics of independence and stand psychologically alone.

Finally—on tribalism—you must know that tribalism appeals to the mind and not to the emotions. But 'reason', i.e. accurate thinking is outlawed by tribalism, as well, because it would uncover tribalism's contradictions and show its falseness. So, tribalism is a 'contradictory' mind philosophy which declares true feelings are invalid. "Keep your feelings denied and exist in your mental center only without the benefits of the moral truth, and, don't stand alone, give into others, because, "if you don't I will murder you", says the power tripper.

This would have great appeal for anyone who doesn't want to deal with his feelings since it denies the feelings as valid from the outset. This is why the majority of people 'went' for tribalism. God knew that mankind had to go this route in order to learn what life is like without reason and free will, so, man could see just why these two are necessary. That time is over and now is the time to embrace the will by embracing reason, individual rights and independence instead of staying a tribalist living in the 'shelter' of the tribe.

The summary on the nature of being (who you are) is to say being is a five part entity: spirit/mental part; will/emotion part; heart/love (acceptance) part, body/sight part; and conscious/subconscious part. This description includes the basic nature of all beings in creation including God's nature.

It is the possession of each of these five parts **in some degree** that all life forms are made up of, be it a mosquito or a man as two examples. Isn't this a simply glorious delineation and such a sweeping identification? The simplicity of the essence of the truth about reality is like this and I hope to show you other basic facts of the same order throughout this book.

There are five basic powers of being, then: 1 **reason** or accurate thinking, deals with thoughts; 2 **freedom** or morality and values; although discovered by the mind, it is utilized by the will/emotions in dealing with feelings in order to tell the self whether things are for it or against it; 3 **love** or acceptance is dealt with by the heart center; 4 **beauty** or visual acuity by the body, deals with pictures and form; 5 **harmony** is the job of the conscious/subconscious and deals with balancing these previous four energies in a harmonious manner.

Knowing that these five powers are the main features of being you can begin to recognize and develop each of them—which will start you on the road to self realization. Take an inventory, through introspection, of where each one of your five energies is at and you will get the beginning point to bring them more fully into fruition. One reason you may want to do this is because ecstasy is the payoff and you are learning to be all you were meant to be.

*   *   *

CHAPTER TWO
On Good and Evil

What is good?

The bottom line truth of what is good and what is evil can be stated as: good is the establishment of those conditions that allow for the individual to live in accordance with his nature—a free, feeling, thinking, soveirgn being. Evil, then, is the obstruction of the individual to do this.

This translates into two different philosophies: the (psychologically) dead philosophy of tribalism on the one hand; and the living philosophy of independence and free will on the other hand. The requirements of man's nature demand the philosophy of independence to be upheld for his fulfillment. The truth of the philosophy of tribalism exposes it to be the false philosophy, abhorrent to the well being of man—it's actually a system designed to kill the will/feelings because it then eliminates the need to deal with the emotions of fear, rage and grief that reside in each of us.

I said earlier that the predominant philosophy the world over is power-trip tribalism. This philosophy has roots that go way back through history to its beginning and has had dominance all of this time in all societies of the peoples of earth. This is not surprising to learn if you realize that the creation's evolution man is engaged in is that of will denial i.e. denial of the feelings. It is exactly the truth of the philosophy of independence that was denied because this is the philosophy that allows for the will/feelings. Tribalism has always been accepted and is accepted to this day exactly because it denies the will/feelings.

Logically then, if you begin to practice the philosophy of independence you are allowing your will to come out of denial since the will is so related to ethics. This is great news because it shows the way to heal the self: **Uphold the ethics of independence and this will allow the will to live.** However, there are two problems with this that needs to be looked at.

One problem you will face if you start this process of accepting free will is others will not like this at all. They will pull out their arsenal of orders, guilt trips, fear trips and hate trips, of which they think is the ultimate power, and will use them against you. You can, perhaps, see that it is the tribalist philosophy that is embraced by most people because it denies the will, and the reason they want to deny the will is because they don't want to deal with 'lost will' that is resident in each of us. Lost will is composed of fear, rage and grief and is held in denial in the subconscious.

Ignorance of true good and evil is one factor that explains, in part, the tribalist psychology. However, it remains to be the truth that instead of reaching for the true ethics of free will most people choose to uphold tribalism and power tripping, and then lie to themselves that tribalism is right. So what this means is they would rather do evil, via using power trips, and believe in the philosophy of tribalism than feel their own will/feelings and live in the truth of independence. That is only the half of it though; **they will also use their power trips on anyone else doing free will.** This entire scenario is backed up by murderous blaming rage for anyone pursuing this course of free will—'that is worst case scenario'. The basic reason this is taking place is because living with the feelings is such an awesomely huge task.

In God's channeled books received by Ceanne De Rohan he gives the essential description of our denial evolution but it is not the purpose of this book to give much information on this. I can tell you, however, that what evolution boils down to is that we are holding rage, fear and grief in our subconscious, from original imprinting and from our past experiences with tribalism; and we are not accepting nor expressing these three emotions with healing intent—they are actively denied by most of us as a matter of course in our everyday lives. The denial of the will is taking place expressly to deny these feelings; the denial of individual rights/independence is taking place for the same reason. If we would get in touch with these emotions and accept and express them over and over again, a little at a time, with healing intent and without violating the rights of others in the process, we would heal them a little at a time. Practicing the ethics of independence will facilitate this. It is also true, to have acceptance for these emotions is exactly what will facilitate practicing the ethics of independence. So, do one and you allow for the other.

Self Sovereignty

There is one principle the ethics of independence upholds as the guiding light of social interaction between people. If you constantly hold this one sacred truth and learn not to violate it you will achieve social guiltlessness. The principle is 'each person must be regarded as a **soveirgn individual** that runs his own life as he sees fit, not as you see fit for him'. An implication of this principle is: 'you should **never initiate power trips** against another. The most common way that people power trip others is to use orders, guilt trips, fear trips and hate trips on him and these are usually done when he, the victim, is in the free will state. These can be given by body language, innuendos, telepathy or words; they range from being very subtle to being glaringly obvious. Remember this is being done in order to hurt your feelings so that you will give up feelings, free will and the independence ethics—tribalists can't stand for anyone to be free, as I have said earlier.

However, one benefit of following this principle is this will free you up to focus on your own life more and what is going on with you. Even when you have interactions with others and you respect this principle, your relations with others—provided they do the same—will work out as they should and you'll be morally perfect. This is the way people were meant to be with each other and this is consonant with human nature and with free will.

In this world of switching definitions and words with rubber meanings and misinformation being mixed up with true understandings until you cant tell them apart, especially in the realm of the humanities, it is a welcome relief to know that there are certain truths that will always be true and that even though others may try to invalidate them with semantics or double talk they remain unassailable. This principle of self sovereignty is this way and is so rock-solid it defies defamation.

Another fact that supports this principle of self sovereignty is that we are Gods and Goddesses in evolution. Common sense, then, reveals that each person should be regarded as soveirgn. God has evolved into the truth of free will and he states that his will is not in opposition to each individual's will, i.e. he is validating this principle also.

Before recent times, the idea of doing your own will was to be dropped in favor of doing Gods will, or your despots will, or your neighbors will. This idea is passé and although held by most of the humanities to this day, it is false. The reason it was endorsed in the first place was because it short circuited the will of which the tribalist ethics were against. The reasons they were and still are against the will is because they don't want to deal with the fear, rage and grief resident in the will (as I've said earlier) and they don't want to go against the social order of tribalism.

Already in this talk on good and evil I have stated a profound point of difference between the true ethics of independence and the false ethics of tribalism—self sovereignty being right and its denial being wrong, i.e. you have the right to live for your own benefit provided you respect this same right of others. In a very real sense, then, along with respecting the rights of others, you should practice rational self interest—ask constantly 'what is in it for me?' Don't use others in this process and you will be right on.

What I want to highlight on this subject is that by following the ethics of free will you will be morally right for reality and once you see that the net of tribalism is using **false guilt** on you, i.e. you know its false, the guilt problem is mostly taken care of, however, your fear, rage and grief around this issue is going to come up for processing.

You are going to want to rage at them for upholding the death philosophy of tribalism and wanting to kill you, psychologically, because you do free will. You are going to experience fear because you will begin to understand that what they are doing is summed up under the identification of 'hatred of the good for being good'. You will feel grief because this state of tribalism is the 'status quo' of the peoples of the world. Feel and express these three emotions again and again to heal them until you express all the emotional charge you have **in response to learning and holding the truth about good and evil.** Realize that tribalism is on the way out— and continue to carry on with following freedom, feeling, rational self concern and self soveirgnty. You have much fear, rage and grief inside you but I am asking you to only deal with the amount of these three emotions you have **in response** to accepting the truth about morality. **Notice that the accepting and expressing of these emotions are the actions of healing them.** Also, remember, that God is on your side in this process

The nature of the opposition to free will

The next point I want to make is the fact that above all else the tribalist is a **moralist** (for tribalism). Since he needs to deny his own will/feelings because of the rage, fear and grief resident there from original imprinting that he doesn't know how to deal with, and because he doesn't want to go against the status quo of tribalism, he has duped himself into believing that tribalism is the true morality. Because of this he has actually convinced himself that tribalism is good and that free will is evil. Then, because of this decision to uphold tribalism he went the next step and adopted the belief that it is also moral to power trip others in the name of tribalism. Taking this stand he subconsciously knows he can keep his will in denial and simultaneously fool himself into believing he is moral. If he was to learn the truth that tribalism is in fact immoral he would then have to face his emotions and go against the tribalist majority. This is something he does not want or know how to do.

Earlier, in his past, the alternative that he wordlessly faced as a child was: 1. Adopt tribalism because it denies the feelings and others have adopted it, or 2. Live in the truth of free will/independence and deal with the feelings and go against the crowd. His choice, in most cases, was 'adopt the ethics of tribalism, go with the crowd and give up the will'. The key point here is that the tribalist does not have this knowledge of why he chose tribalism but, never-the-less, this is the reason he has done so. He has convinced himself that tribalism is moral and because of this he will not give it up in favor of the truth of free will easily.

However, it remains to be true that the **primary weapon** of the tribalist is **morality.** If you learn that the truth of true good is independence, reason, free will and self interest you will also find out that the tribalist is practicing the false morality of tribalism. In order for you to know this **you will have to know good and evil completely**—which is what I am teaching in this book. Once you master morality you may wonder how the tribalist could fall for such a shabby system of good and evil like tribalism. That system serves its purpose of killing the will and that is why he buys into it.

It is also true that tribalism can't withstand the power of true moral reasoning because that would show it to be false. What this means then, is people who buy into it have killed their power of reason in the realm of morality when they believed tribalism was true. It's actually a contradiction of the facts of reality being held as the truth. Holding this contradiction, I believe, 'short circuits' the minds ability to know anything clearly; and if this is true, the tribalist is a 'dummy'.

Isn't it something that for a person to live in today's world of tribalism he must learn true good and evil because if he doesn't he is prey to all the tribalists that uphold false good and evil? In other words one of the

23

costs of truly living is, you must learn the truth about good and evil i.e. the truth of the two morality systems. The tribalist is right in his dedication to morality but wrong in the moral system he chose—his morality is the death morality. The free person should hold as strong a dedication to the truth of the free will morality.

The essence of the tribalist

I now want to give you the summary of the immoral majority of which I have been speaking. **In a sentence, the people who are evil are: 'tribalists, mentalists and power trippers**—this is their bottom line.

They are **tribalists** because 1. They don't want to go against the others who uphold tribalism and 2. They gave up their feelings because they don't want to deal with them (tribalism denies the will/feelings). This adopted, false ethics of tribalism jettisons them out of their own feelings and forces them to live in their mental center only, but true reasoning is their enemy also because it would lead to the truth that free will and independence are true….. and tribalism is false.

They are **mentalists** with their will denied. Actually they are contorting their thinking to somehow make tribalism appear to be true but since it is false this is an impossibility—this doesn't daunt them none-the-less; it's reminiscence of a dog trying to catch his tail but never quite succeeds. All because living with the feelings and going against the majority is something they don't want or know how to do.

They are **power trippers** that have to attack anyone who practices free will/independence. They cannot allow a single person in their presence to be free; they have to force tribalism on anyone doing so. To do this they use orders, guilt trips, fear trips and hate trips, however, the foundation of their stand against free will........ is morality. They hold that **free will is wrong** and if they didn't believe you were wrong for doing free will they would never power trip you. But, free will is not wrong—it is the true good and it is a crying shame that most people viciously attack this in anyone who practices it. I hope to show you how to deal successfully with 'mister power tripper' as this book continues.

To make it believable so they can deny the will, the tribalists have a set of lies (contradictions) that portray tribalism and power tripping as being good. This rationalization structure is necessary and indispensable to them because of the fact of the principle that **'man has the need to know he is right'**—its part of his nature. This means that the tribalist has adopted a set of false beliefs which actually whitewashes tribalism and gives him the illusion that tribalism is true, good and moral.

I said earlier that the main problem on earth is power trip tribalism and I have just given you a list of facts describing what the tribalist is doing and why he is doing it. It has been this scenario that has been operative throughout past history and has caused all the ethical/political structures that have existed—except for America, that is, with its Constitution and Bill of Rights. This is the target for modern day, power tripping politicians and they know that they can't establish a dictatorship, (political tribalism), without destroying these two documents.

You have the truth on your side when you uphold independence as the good and if you learn how to live this, you are living in the moral truth and are no longer plagued by true guilt. The reason why the tribalist had power in the first place is because we, the independence/ free will supporters didn't have the truth of the morality of free will and so we conceded that he, the tribalist, was 'somehow right' and that we just didn't understand it. (I learned that from Ayn Rand). Armed with the truth of good and evil we now know that his morality is false. This knowledge alone is enough to enable you to not buy into this false system of morality, where before, he had the advantage because we sidestepped the realm of morality when he did not.

You can feel heartened however because this viewpoint I'm delineating here shows you exactly the 'what' and 'why' of tribalism so you are no longer in the dark about it. Since evolution's problems are seen clearly, we have the understandings to heal them and attain true happiness. Whether you believe in a higher power or not, all of us can agree that reason and freedom/individual rights are necessary for mans fulfillment and happiness on earth.

Murderous blaming rage against the free will state

My next topic is the delineation of the two major states of consciousness that people can occupy. The first state is the psychologically living state of 'think and feel' (reason and free will); the second state is the psychologically dead state of 'think only' (but not necessarily in the truth) and don't feel. The first is the state of self soveirgnty and the second is the tribal state of consciousness—in denial of true thinking and feeling.

In the truth, the independent one—the 'think/feel' state—is morally correct and the tribalist state of 'think only' is morally incorrect because he denies his will and reason, (however, the tribalist believes it's the other way around). These two states are the two morally significant states and the battle takes place here between the two of them.

When you get into the state of 'think and feel'(reason and free will), in the presence of another, this will more than likely trigger him to get into his 'mind only' tribal state and attack you with his false morality. The **worst case scenario** is he will attack you with murderous blaming rage.

Each of us has an imprint in the subconscious that, in essence, amounts to the mental level being programmed to murderously kill the feeling level either in regards to the self or in regard to others doing free will. This imprint is full of murderous hatred and blaming rage and because no-one knew what was going on here everyone stayed away from free will since this triggered this murderous rage in others.

This murderous blaming rage can easily be triggered by anyone doing free will and you will have to be attentive not to trigger this in others as you go about your day in this up state of free will. Don't go past me on this and think it is not much of a problem because it is the most serious problem you will have to face in the realm of relationships with others. It is my belief that because free will triggers this "gap" where murderous hatred resides in others that this is one of the major reasons why no one, thru the past, wanted to do free will.

A solution to this is to try not to trigger this in others by not doing free will in their presence. Become a pro at getting in and out of this 'up state' of free will so you can safely navigate in the dangerous waters of the opposition of others. As far as how to heal this imprint we all have inside us you must go to God's channeled books to Ceanne De Rohan for full details on this because it is beyond the scope of this book to say much about it. I can say, however, that by you **accepting** your fear, rage and grief and give all three of these feelings **expression**, without dumping on others in this process, you will heal them in this way, a little at a time.

Since everyone denies especially these three feelings, these feelings are forced to exist outside of our acceptance in each us and this is the problem. You can know also that because we have denied these three feelings since time began we were forced into the ethics of tribalism as a means of shutting them down so they wouldn't be a problem. Now, the knowledge of **accepting** these three emotions is exactly what will heal them and will thus allow us to live in the truth of reason, free will and independence. Begin accepting them a little at a time as your capacity permits. As you begin to understand and practice reason and free will you will experience these emotions coming up for acceptance in this process so allow them to surface and stop yourself from feeling them only when they get overwhelming.

The free will state

Now I want to give you the 'mechanics' of doing free will. This state I'm going to describe to you is so very valuable because in it you can **practically** gain a state of joy and moral perfection.

If you are practicing the virtue called 'independence' (from others), others will not be able to bring you down with their power trips because you are relying on yourself only and you are psychologically separate from them. If you are also not initiating power tripping others, you are guilt free. With these two conditions met you can enter into this up state of being. This state is such a glorious state that when you get into it you feel wonderful and in this state you really **live** your life. I will now define this state for the purpose of you being able to call it up at will.

The goal is to have all five of your energies that make you up, in an 'online' state. Thus: 'reason' alive for your mind; will focused in 'feeling free and monitoring right and wrong; heart in a state of 'self acceptance' (unconditional love); body 'seeing the beauty of physical reality'; consciousness balancing these other four harmoniously. In short I call these powers, **reason, freedom, love, beauty** and **harmony**.

Two steps you can perform to get into this up state are: 1. be aware of your eyes seeing 'beautiful real' of your physical surroundings; and 2. hold the idea that it's moral for you to 'go for it for yourself'. To be aware in this state, coax your eyes to see the objects around as being 'real' and 'beautiful'. Concurrently, with your eyes seeing this 'is ness' of things, you hold the thought 'I go for it for what I can get out of the moment but never hurting others in the process', you will jump into this higher state. I can call this state up any time I want in this way and I feel it will work for you as well. In fact it is so potent that I have to cool things down by doing it sparingly until I get used to it.....Non-the-less, what a delightful task!

You possess these five powers of being and you can get each one into their 'up state' separately in order to get the 'feel' for each of them. Then when you learn to get all of them 'up', the resultant state is **ecstasy itself.** Mind and will are balancing in the heart, and body is seeing the truth of physical reality's beauty; your conscious/subconscious energy is balancing these four—this is the proper relationship of your five energies to each other.

So, the conscious-subconscious energy has the job of being conscious of the other four consciousnesses and maintaining balance. For example, if you focus on what your eyes are seeing with your body energy, and then have this 'orchestrator' be conscious of the consciousness of your eyes seeing, this could 'pop' you into the up state of your body energy. Doing the same thing with the other three energies can get them 'up' as well. You can then recognize the sublime beauty and joy of this state of 'consciousness of your energies up state'. Being conscious of consciousness as I have just described is an awesome state of being and once you experience it you will not want anything less.

Doing these things will put you in this higher state of awareness, as I have said, and being in the moment like this becomes a 'blast'—a whole lot of fun. So, in one moment you are in a lesser state of awareness and things look dull and lifeless. You then work your eyesight to focus on the 'beautiful realness' of your surroundings and that you are real also. Next you reaffirm that it's right for you to live for your own benefit and 'at the same time' activate your attention to be conscious of your consciousness—in this case it's your seeing. Presto, your awareness jumps up into this higher state and you feel free and happy. With myself I use this technique any time I want and get the joy of this higher awareness state.

The payoffs from doing this are many. One immediate benefit is that in this state, since you are living your life and not others lives, if and when they power trip you, which they will certainly do, it doesn't phase you because you don't have life with them—you don't depend on them for you to do this—instead you rely on yourself and you are psychologically independent of all others. Another payoff is, the joy of being in this state is well worth doing so. Yet another payoff is the satisfaction you will receive from doing this because you are really **living** your life.

A good idea in practicing this higher state of awareness that may help is for you to listen to yourself only and not others. I mean, your goal is to be a self sufficient being standing on your own two feet, ideally, in all matters of life.

As far as how to deal with others I would just caution you to not sacrifice your own psychological state of 'living', for another. This won't accomplish anything because it's not moral and will result in you die-ing to your own self independence and joy i.e. **life is a singular activity.** If you want to help others tell them how to do this higher state of awareness I'm talking about.

For all you 'loners' out there this practice should be 'right up your alley' since you have fewer relations with others. You probably have fewer relationships because you sense that most people are power trippers against anyone who enters the free will state. Remember that your relationship with yourself is the primary concern and your relationship with others is second.

In this 'up' state you are mainly concerned with what you are doing and you let others do whatever they want to do, be it power trip you or not it doesn't matter because since your focus is mainly on yourself their power trips are like water rolling off a duck's back. You know right from wrong and you are right because you are not power tripping anyone in this state, i.e. you respect this same right in others, so, you are morally guiltless and this means that you are right—**morally right for reality**! I mean, what's the point in power tripping? Power trips are interactions with others in a way that takes you out of rational self life i.e. you are wasting your time with mixing it up with others in this way instead of living your own precious life. What's more, if you do power trip others you get guilt every time you do it and that could affect you adversely. Anyway, this state is so satisfying that it is really all you would ever want to do. This is the ultimate state of 'living' and if you could invoke it at will you will have your happiness at your command—by simply getting into this living state. I will talk more on this in chapter five.

Remember that you must rely on yourself only to maintain this state of joy, and not rely on others at all. I mean, when you accomplish this self reliance, others can power trip you but it has little effect because you are sailing in known waters and your psychological independence protects you from their attacks, however, by you gaining mastery of this state—being able to turn it on and off—you can safely traverse these dangerous waters by getting out of the state until the danger subsides.

I have been practicing this 'up state' a lot lately and I find it continuously enjoyable. I plan to practice it from now on—as I desire. Along with practicing this state you must not initiate power tripping others or interfere with others lives in any way. This will keep you socially guiltless and allow you to live in this moral truth of independence. When you try this out you will find that many of your problems you have been having with others will, as if by magic, disappear. The statement that names what you are doing is "I **live** my life by living for my own benefit and others are free of my interference in their lives".

What in the world is going on?

What is really going on is the ethics of tribalism are established on earth and nearly all people follow them. What this means, practically, is that **everyone is hurting everyone else's feelings** with order trips, guilt trips, fear trips and hate trips. These trips are launched against anyone entering the state of free will, reason and independence. These trips are a necessity to the tribal ethics and their goal is to keep the feelings and the moral truth dead—in themselves and in you.

What should be going on is each of us should live for the self's own benefit; live each his/her own life and quit trying to force others into obeying the false ideas of right and wrong upheld by the tribalists; and, respect this same right in others—and cease the power trips against the feelings and reason. (This is the criteria of utopia!) This also means that everyone should accept the feelings of fear, rage and grief instead of denying them with power trips (easier said than done); and, maintain moral perfection by realizing, power tripping, overpowering others or others overpowering you, is wrong.

Surely you can see that in today's environment, as throughout the past, it's been the will/feelings that have been the target of the power trips. The message everyone receives from these power trips is that "the feelings are neither allowed nor wanted and are to be denied in order to get along with others".

Now, the burning question is: Why is the denial of the feelings taking place in the first place? Denial of the feelings is the type of evolution the entire creation is involved in that answers this question. Beings, you, me and GOD, have been in denial of the feelings because it is the feelings that are the heaviest to deal with since they include fear/terror, anger/rage, pain and grief.

Ethically, the denial of the feelings that tribalism upholds is the system of the past and the ethics of independence is the system of the future. God's evolution is now to the point that he is not denying his feelings anymore and so we must begin accepting our feelings and the consequent ethics of individual rights. This is a very 'tall order' but it seems that if we don't do this, 'lost will' (the feelings we deny) may take the entire creation down into extinction. Just how we can do this is the topic of His eight books he sent to earth via Ceanne DeRohan. In this

book I show all about the two ethical systems and give pointers on how to accept the feelings of the will that is present with you now. God shows how to heal your being completely in Ceanne's books.

So the goal of creation is to bring all of the feelings out of denial and heal them thru acceptance and love. Concurrently we must embrace reason and individual rights. Doing these things will restore our immortality and land us in the New Age of Aquarius!

This then, Ladies and Gentlemen is the overview of what is truly going on in the world!

*   *   *

A few days ago it occurred to me that the tribal state of being is a 'group' oriented state. In other words the relationship of self to others is elevated above the relationship of self to self. It's also plain to me that this group orientation denies the will/feelings in each person involved in it. The point I want to make is that there are two distinct states of being; 1 free will/independent state and 2 the tribal (group) state.

In viewing most people, the reason it has been so hard for me to 'see' them is because most people practice both states; they are tribalistic some of the time and they are independent at other times. Since people do not know the difference they don't know what to promote in themselves and what to inhibit. So, we have the spectacle of a person coming across as a free person but then he lays a power trip on you from the tribalist state, thinking it is alright to do so, and then jumps back into the free will state.

God said that free will is not established on earth yet; and what this means is that tribalism **is** established instead. This equates to the fact that when you get into this state of free will you will get power tripped extensively by those you are in the presence of. To deal with them you will have to know right and wrong completely and you will have to maintain psychological independence from all others.

Some people will express extreme hatred at you for doing this state. When they do this to me I have decided that although they hate me for being good I hate them more for being bad. You have the 'dirty rats' dead to true good and hating you for it and you can know therefore that they are wrong.

The fear trip doesn't come at me very much lately but earlier I had to deal with it also. I accepted my fear and allowed it expression and acceptance and got used to feeling it and now the fear is no big deal for me—I mean I could only feel a certain amount of fear about the status quo of tribalism and as I processed this fear through acceptance and expression, I no longer had fear about tribalism and 'the hatred of the good for being good' which it implied. At first you will feel this fear because you are 'looking at the naked face of evil'. Great, accept it and express it until you can accept that tribalism is truly the death philosophy 'out to get you'.

The order trip is the most blatantly wrong power trip because it tries to kill your free will by them trying to boss you around instead of leaving you free to lead your own life the way you see fit and not as they see fit. Remember that as you practice this free will state you must maintain independence of others and therefore be out of the reach of their power trips.

The guilt trip they will throw at you can be dealt with firstly by you mastering the truth of good and evil. Once this is accomplished you know that he is using false guilt on you and you know why he is using it—will denial—because of lost will inside each of us. Also remember to maintain your independence and it will have no affect on you as well.

The essence of the opposition to free will

The way man is designed to function is to say he needs to be free and independent. When he is being independent of all others and pursuing moral desires he is necessarily happy. I will call this state 'free' consciousness. Now, the power tripper does not want to allow anyone to be in this 'free state'. He is not in the 'free state' himself and he is against anyone who is. The power tripper is in what I call 'master/slave' consciousness. This is a tribal state of consciousness and it is dead set against anyone in the 'free state'. As you try out this 'free state' you will encounter the master/slave state of consciousness of the others around you and they will use orders, guilt trips, fear trips and hate trips to break you of this free state.

In order for you to successfully deal with him you must first realize that he is in this state of 'master/slave' consciousness and that this is an immoral state. Technically, since he is trying to make you his slave every time you are in the free state, he is breaking cosmic law which states 'you can do what you want provided you don't overpower others in the process'—you go for it for yourself and respect that same right in others. So, in power tripping you, he is morally wrong and you have the moral advantage over him. You must also know that he has whitewashed his power-trip behavior with rationalizations and believes that he is morally right. But his reasons for believing power tripping is good, are false. If you were to realize this fact when he is attacking you when you are in the free will state you will be able to use the truth of this to not buy into the power trip. Besides, if you were to maintain psychological independence of all others then his trips would have little or no effect on you. Remember also that the human race had to experience tribalism to learn what evil is, so this is an evolutionary state of affairs. Further, the time has come, in man's evolution, for all people to drop the false, tribal ethics and begin accepting the true ethics of freewill.

A good piece of advice here is that when all is said and done you should depend on yourself and no-one else for your happiness. If others are hurting you with their power trips then you are not being independent and you are bought into 'other-ism'. I have found that when I depend on myself only and do not let others influence me whatsoever, I have control of my life and it is joyful. Then, when and if they power trip me it is like water running off a duck's back in that it has no effect.

What is the reason you would want to go against the status quo of tribalism and pursue this path of freedom? I will answer this simply by saying that when you achieve the beginning states of 'free consciousness', by working with the ideas in this book, you will see that it is such a glorious, wonderful and right way to be that you will want, for these reasons, to work to maintain it. Really, it's one of the 'golden' goals of maturing into the moral truth of free will. Also, just wait to see how much fun it is and that it is wholly possible to maintain it day after day. In short, by mastering the knowledge of good and evil you can achieve your own happiness and you will see the way life was always meant to be.

CHAPTER THREE
The System

It is my pleasure to now delineate a set of principles—there are only five—that will insure your happiness throughout your day to day existence if you constantly remember them and follow them….. I call this **'The System'**.

The principles are:
1. Independence
2. Mind your own business (live your life, not others lives)
3. Don't misjudge
4. Don't initiate power trips against others
5. Accept fear rage and grief

Independence means you are psychologically independent of all others. You depend on yourself only, to maintain your balance of your consciousness. Your relationship with others should be as independent beings, each living from his/her own resources. When you practice this principle you are protected against others powers tripping you simply because you are being independent of others and the trips have little effect on you i.e. you live from your own resources which don't depend on what others do.

Mind your own business means that you live **your** life and that you realize full well that others have to live their life also. You should nurture your relationship with yourself because it is this relationship that is of cardinal importance to your being ness and is 'part and parcel' of living your life. You don't want to give up your own sense of self to become 'one' with the group and follow group pursuits not of your choosing. You can take part in cooperative endeavors with others but do it being independent and be mostly concerned with yourself and your actions.

With this principle you have two conditions in which to practice this: when you are not in the presence of others; and when you are in the presence of others. It may be easier to do this when you are alone and this is a good place to start but relations with others is a big part of life also and so learning to balance yourself when you are with others is important. In conclusion, you are always 'minding your own business', i.e. you are living your life, not other's lives, no matter which conditions you are facing.

When you are living this principle you are practicing that 'you are'—you are saying 'I am'! When you interact with others you should not give up your independence to them and you shouldn't ask them to give up their independence to you. To violate this principle you could become a tribal member by ditching your independence and follow the dictates of a tribal leader (psychologically) but this would be immoral.

Minding your own business also means you are living for your own benefit. After all you are the actor so you should gain the benefit from your actions. Anything else would entail self sacrifice which is abhorrent to the well being of the individual.

In the work place the reason working at a job functions so well is because each person performs effortful actions for an employer in exchange for monetary value. This system of just compensation is at the root of capitalism—and is moral—in accordance with the principle of everyone living for himself.

There is so much ecstasy that is available to you when you take this principle to the heights of practice, that it is hard to describe. When your consciousness increases to include the rightness of self awareness, i.e. you realize it was always meant for you to be 'super self concerned' and that all you owed others was to not interfere with them, you can enter the hallways of self realization and once you experience this state you will never want to backslide into tribalism ever again.

"Don't misjudge" means you are keeping your mind locked into the truth. I use the word misjudgment to mean a 'pseudo identification' of any aspect of reality you are thinking on. Usually misjudgments have a kernel of truth that make them believable but also, necessarily, contain contradictions. Misjudgments are always false and for you to hold a misjudgment actually extracts your mind out of the truth on the issue you made it on.

When I first began practicing this principle I discovered I had a whole slue of misjudgments I was holding and by me monitoring what I thought of things, I weeded out my misjudgments as they came up to my attention. I still make misjudgments in my daily life but I always recognize them and discard them as false. As you do this same work with yourself you will become clearer and clearer until you will reach a peace in your mind that previous to this, misjudgments made impossible to attain. In a word, your mind is 'clean' because it is free of misjudgments. In a person that holds a lot of misjudgments, the mind is in turmoil because the denied truth and the misjudgments are in conflict with each other. Recognizing when you misjudge is a big part of balancing in this system and so you must be able to know when you are misjudging and when you are discerning.

'Discerning' is the correct and true way of thinking and is misjudgment free. Discerning names facts of reality and follows the rules of reason. For you to determine when you are misjudging and when you are discerning is paramount to practicing this system. Without this knowledge the system will not work for you.

A good way to recognize misjudgments is, 'misjudgments see the situation as never changing'. An example of a misjudgment is: a person rages at you unjustly and it hurts your feelings. You then form the misjudgment that this guy is a jerk and that you will maintain this misjudgment until 'kingdom comes'. If you were discerning the situation instead of misjudging it you would know that this is, perhaps, an isolated action and that you feel resentment toward him; because of this resentment you misjudged him. The bad part about this scenario is that by your misjudgment you have just extracted your mind out of the realm of truth on this issue (by endorsing the misjudgment). Consequently you are also the loser because you're truth structure has been compromised by the misjudgment.

In my current experience I continue to form misjudgments many times each day—they just pop up from my subconscious—but since I know how to recognize them I almost always catch them and label them as misjudgments. With this recognition I discard them and they have no effect on me. In order to know if you are misjudging or discerning, ask yourself if your thoughts on the aspect of reality you are focused on, 'name that tune'. Think in terms of specific definitions that get to the 'bottom line' knowledge of what you're considering.

Another nice thing about learning this discrimination is that your subconscious will then be able to bring up to your awareness, misjudgments you have made in the past in order for you to correct your thinking by recognizing them as such, with the use of reason.

Don't power trip others means you know that power trips are the weapon of the tribal ethics and that the purpose of the power trips is to attack the free will of the independence practitioners and thereby force them to concede that tribalism is correct. By you not initiating power trips on others you are being socially moral and this is one of the criteria of the independence ethics. When you stop initiating power trips on others you are eliminating true guilt and as a result of this you will reclaim your innocence.

Accept fear, rage and grief means you are not denying your feelings any longer because you know that denying them caused the problem of evolution, within each of us, in the first place. Denying the feelings is exactly why the tribal ethics were and still are embraced by most people. Accept the feelings, predominantly the fear, rage and grief, a little at a time until you get used to them, then; gradually allow them to be felt more and more. The denial of theses feelings is exactly

47

what everyone does and to accept them is exactly the **healing action** they need.

OK, fine, these are the principles but what do you do with them? In order for these principles to be of use to you, you must first see their value as the most perfect truths of moral being-ness. Next, if you want to use this system, you must memorize these principles such that they actually become automatic in your consciousness so you can call them up from your subconscious at any time of the day.

So, in summary: I maintain independence; I live my life (I mind my own business); I don't misjudge; I don't initiate power trips on others; I feel. By constantly remembering these principles I kind of monitor, mainly myself, and to a lesser degree, the people around me, to see if these principles are being obeyed or violated. The moral truth is that everyone on earth should never violate these principles and if you or they do so, you or they are acting immoral.

The main violation of people is power tripping the one who is doing free will. This is the single most common way to violate another's right to life and independence. If you choose to practice this system you will undoubtedly draw others to initiate power trips against you. When they do this, you can know that they are dead wrong and are acting immoral. Because you know that all power trips aim at hurting your feelings you know what is being protected by following the principle of independence; you also know that your main concern is yourself so, what others do is of secondary concern. If you are feeling hurt from their power trips then I suggest that you are not maintaining your independence. So, remember, to protect you from others attacks, is the main purpose of following the independence principle.

Misjudging reality instead of discerning reality is a big drawback in itself and so you must be able to learn this discrimination. As you practice this principle you will see first hand the great importance of it— not misjudging eliminates a whole gross of problems that would otherwise grow from the fertile ground of misjudgments.

There is not much you can do to prevent others from misjudging you but you can at least recognize their misjudgments if and when they become apparent to you.

When you practice this system, you are being morally perfect, your mind is misjudgment free and peaceful, you are independent and focused on your life, and you are respecting this same right to life in others by not power tripping them nor misjudging them. The wonderful and awesome result of this is joy. I not only live in a constant state of happiness when I live this system, I also get approval from many others—most people are smart enough to recognize the rightness of this system and it turns out that my popularity with others is great.

The last principle I listed at the beginning of this chapter is not to deny your emotions. The reason why we have had the experience of tribalism is because we couldn't accept the emotions of the will. Little did anyone know that to accept them and allow them to express is exactly what the will needs to heal itself. As I have said the three most denied emotions are fear, rage and grief. To begin to lovingly accept these three emotions goes along with this system and just as the most needed thing for the mind is recognizing and eliminating misjudgments, the most necessary thing for the will is to stop denying the emotions.

I practice **'the system'** in my day to day life and I find it a wonderful way of being to always come back to. In practicing this system my mind purrs like a kitten because I don't misjudge and I am guilt free because I don't initiate power trips on others. I am also truly living my life and a state of joy results as a consequence. Through explaining this system I offer you a practical way in which to obtain your happiness right here and right now.

People, in general, are sometimes good and sometimes bad. Even though they don't know it they sometimes live in accordance with this system and sometimes they violate it. What this means to someone who knows 'the system' is, one can see when others are good and when they are bad.

It is my understanding that 'if people knew better they would do better'. So, the main problem, then, is that the **knowledge** of good and evil is not known by most people but if it were known by them they would gladly practice it no matter what the cost since it is what's right.

Can you see that if everyone followed this system we would have a society of heaven on earth—an actual utopia? In the Age of Aquarius, which is upon us, these are exactly the principles that everyone will know as the ultimate moral truth. When you practice this system you can experience how it is to live in forever.

CHAPTER FOUR
Practical right and wrong

The only two states of being

Knowing, then, that each of us should practice 'the system', at all times of our waking life, and knowing that it comes under our conscious control as a result of understanding how and why to do so, we can practice it at will—any time we want.

Whether we know it or not we all practice 'the system' sometimes during our day to day living but we also violate it at other times. Because we didn't have the knowledge of true right and wrong, before now, we sometimes did right and sometimes did wrong, in this manner, but never knew the difference. But, what is the state we get into when we are not doing 'the system'?

This is a state we adopted early in life as a child, when, at which time, most of us decided to go with the crowd and give up free will and moral thinking. In this state power tripping others is seen as OK since it is in the name of what's good—tribalism's good. Also, the will is denied in this state and emphasis is placed instead on the mental side of being; but, misjudgemental thinking is king and thinking in reason's truth is frowned upon. Yet another characteristic of this state is to say that we are convinced tribalism is true and good and just as much convinced that reason, freewill and independence are false and evil.

The fact is that the tribalist is living in defiance of the **true morality** of **independence** and since he upholds the tribalist system of right and wrong, his mind becomes impotent because he is holding contradictions to the truth. However, he knows how to power trip expertly and this is what he uses in day to day life to deal with others. He is a moralist for tribalism and claims adamantly that tribalism is the truth. He is constantly on the lookout for people who display any sign of free will, truth, or independence. When he spots one of them he is first to power trip him and make him tow the line of tribalism by exercising his power trip muscles of 'orders, guilt trips, fear trips and hate trips', which target the victim's feelings, and is named "pressure" by many people. He adheres to tribalism for the sole reason it keeps the will denied—he doesn't want to feel and he doesn't want anyone else to feel.

Obviously, the tribalist is holding the misjudgments of tribalism in his mind instead of the true understandings of freedom. Any true understandings he does have, are mixed up with the contradictions (misjudgments), of the tribalist ethics and he doesn't know the difference. This hampers the working of his mind and causes mental disharmony.

In summary, I can say that this alternate state is defined as his, (the tribalist's) mental energy is sunk into the ethics of tribalism and his will is denied. Where, instead of this, he should be embracing reason's truth and the ethics of freedom—independence. In short, he should practice 'the system' at all times of his waking life.

The best way to remember this alternate state is to see that it is the **opposite** state of 'the system'. Instead of independence, i.e. standing alone, psychological ties with others are made; instead of true thinking, misjudgments are upheld; instead of not power tripping, power trips are seen as OK and are used to keep the will down; instead of minding his own business he is focused on others; finally, his emotions are held in denial.

I must tell you that when you do 'the system' people are not going to like this and since their philosophy is tribalism they will launch orders, guilt trips, fear trips and hate trips against you.

When you do 'the system' you will eliminate a lot of conflict inside you but you will become the target of the 'net of tribalism'. Before doing this system, you got along with others, perhaps, because you weren't going against tribalism, but you were unfulfilled inside yourself. So, naturally, for happiness: learn how to do the system; and deal with the power tripping people, who want to stop you.

*   *   *

The bottom line on nearly all the people is that they are guilty of using the power trips as a tool of living. But, they should never use these four (orders, guilt, fear and hate) against anyone. Men women and children, all, are taught to use these trips and I have witnessed the spectacle of a three year old child putting me on a guilt trip for me doing free will in his presence. You can also know that it is this 'alternate state of being' that they are in when they power trip. Great, so what does this mean to the person that wants to practice 'the system'?

If you choose to do this system you have two primary issues you will need to deal with: 1-you must learn how to accept your feelings and 2-you must learn how to deal with the power trippers that want to stop you. Remember it is the feelings they attack in anyone practicing free will or reason.

So let's look at exactly what their attacks against you consist of. Their power trips come in four varieties: orders, guilt trips, fear trips and hate trips, as I have said. Since you master morality you have the guilt trip taken care of since you know true guilt from false guilt and you don't buy into his guilt trips because they are false. If you are accepting your emotions, predominantly the fear, their fear trips are no big deal because fear is no stranger to you. OK fine you are able to deal with these two trips but what about the hate trips and order trips?

You are going to encounter people who will express hatred to you because of you practicing the true good of 'the system'. What's really happening here is the power tripper hates himself because he follows the death philosophy of tribalism and he is transferring his self hatred on to you. He really thinks he hates the good but in reality he has to think he hates you to prevent him from learning, in the truth, its himself he really hates. He hates himself because he is a power tripper. I, personally, really hate the hater, myself but the difference between us is, he hates me for being good but I hate him more for being evil.

That leaves the order trip. He thinks you will obey his orders because if you don't he will use guilt and/or fear trips on you. An order trip implies that he knows what is right for you better than you yourself knows, and that is why this trip hurts—it attacks you living from your own resources and tries to interject the power tripper as a 'significant other' to you. One solution on this is to don't do what he says and communicate to him that you will not obey him until he shows you why you should. So, then, he might bring up a fear trip as his reason for you to obey him. Or, he might bring up a false guilt trip and that that is the reason he will use to make you obey him. In either case he is wrong so tell him, telepathically, to 'kiss off'.

In order to put this knowledge in the right perspective you can realize that this is an evolutionary issue and that mankind needed to experience tribalism and power tripping in order to learn how to accept free will and reason. Next, you can know that in today's world, a great many people are 'moving their butts' to 'get it right'. You can see it on TV and see it in the people around you. At this point in time it is this acknowledged movement that God refers to when he says, and I quote: 'I am very pleased at the movement that the people of earth are making". What this means is that even though the people are still power tripping they are working to understand exactly what is right and loving and how they can get something out of life for themselves and still love their brothers and sisters. In other words we are evolving into the true philosophy of free will, reason, and compassion.

So, when you practice 'the system' and you see the opposition from others, remember this perspective and don't misjudge that, "oh my God, people are evil and there is no changing that". Misjudging exactly that, I, myself, lived in misery as a result of holding the particular misjudgment that, 'I'm being good and everyone else is being evil and that this will never change'. It was only after I realized that I was 'misjudging' this and denying the context 'power tripping' resides in did I release myself from all the pain and misery this misjudgment created.

However, the bottom line of people is that everyone is still a power tripper, including me, to a certain degree. Why, because all the people do not want to feel and they don't want anyone else to feel. That's why the power trips are used—they hurt the will, not the other parts of the being. What we have established, then, in all the societies on earth is a system of 'anti-feel', 'anti-reason' philosophy which is responsible for all the disharmony and misery that is 'par for the course' in the world. The form this tribalism takes is, all the philosophies and religions of the world upholding service to others as the true good—and not individual rights as the ultimate moral truth. The philosophy of Ayn Rand's Objectivism is the notable exception.

The choice, then, boils down to: do you want to start feeling and accept independence as the true morality or; do you want to continue power tripping and living in the false ethics of tribalism? At any rate, there is a saying that goes, 'seeing the problem is half the solution'. So, understanding what I have said and agreeing with it, you're halfway there.

*   *   *

Working on yourself and dealing with others

Supposing, you understand that what I'm saying is true and you want to start living in free will, i.e. the true ethics of independence. How can you do this?

Again, there are two subjects that you must address if you want to live in the moral truth of free will—you must face your feelings, is the first one; the second one is you must learn how to deal with others in a copasetic manner.

Facing your own feelings and allowing them to have presence with you is going to involve feeling the so-called negative emotions, as well as the positive ones. To feel the emotions and to let them express is exactly the healing action the emotions need. You may realize that to deny the emotions is the hallmark of the tribalist and that this constitutes the essence of the major problem of creation. In other words If you want psychological life you will have to accept your feelings during the process of you accepting and practicing individual rights. It is not by coincidence that individual rights and the feelings have both been denied throughout the past. It has always been the denial of the feelings that led to the denial of the ethics of independence. In conclusion, if you do one you will allow the other.

Most of this work of accepting the emotions can go on between you yourself in your own space. Start with understanding and realizing that the moral truth is independence and not tribalism. By 'realizing', I mean 'feeling' the truth of these ethics in your feeling body, (after you have proved them to your mind). When you make these understandings yours, be alert for emotions that will come up, and, allow them to be felt. Fear, rage, and grief will surface, so, see how long you can feel them before you shut them down when they get overwhelming. Remember that every time you feel your emotions in an accepting way, you are healing them a little at a time.

Fine, so you are working to gain the understandings into your mind about ethics, i.e. you are proving to yourself the moral truth and also getting these understandings into your feelings. Next, after practicing feeling the emotions over and over, you are enabling you're self to accept them to a greater and greater degree. You will be getting to know why and what they are. The essence of this situation is that these emotions of fear, rage, and grief have been suppressed all along by all of us since the beginning and is the reason for upholding tribalism. The ultimate goal is to unconditionally accept the will/feelings.

When you accept these understandings to the degree that you can evaluate everything you see, in yourself and the people around you, through the eyes of morality and your tolerance for feeling your emotions has matured into being able to unconditionally accept all your feelings, you will be 'there'—ready for the Age of Aquarius.

You will also, through this process, start to feel the wonderful emotions of joy, and ecstasy as a result of learning to live in the truth and freeing up your will. Remember also to learn how to tell when you are 'misjudging' and when you are 'discerning' reality (misjudgments are always false, as I have said earlier).

So, that is the work to do on yourself but what about dealing with others? As I have said earlier the net of tribalism will rise up against you when you do the system in the presence of others. What is really going on with the power trippers of the net?

The bottom line of the members of the net of tribalism is **they are guilt worshippers.** So, logically, then, they want you to feel false guilt every time you get into the free will state. You see, they think you are wrong, when in reality you are right. It is very easy to be a power tripper and here is what exactly the tribalist is doing: The tribalist spots you doing free will and he right away thinks in his mind that you are wrong and he is right. Then he will start his attacks on you and he will feel justified in doing so because he believes tribalism is right and you doing free will is wrong. Of course the reason he is really against you is because he doesn't want to deal with his feelings and so he has to stop anyone else doing so.

But, the point is that he is setting himself up as a moral superior to you and he claims you are the one who is wrong and he is the one who is right. Anyone can take this stand and it is really easy to do so. Even a three year old who buys into tribalism has this capability and I have seen the little tykes guilt trip me when I do free will in their presence—just like their parents and for the same reason—to deny the feelings.

OK, fine, tribalism is the free will killer ethics and most people will be against you as you practice the independence ethics and begin living with your emotions. A further identification of what is going on with the tribalist is necessary so you can know, exactly, the nature of the opposition you will face.

Inside each of us beings we have 'imprints' that got instilled in us from the beginning times of our evolution. These imprints consist of the mind being imprinted with rage against the will and the will being imprinted with fear of the mind. The heart was imprinted with grief. These imprints have great influence on all of us in our day to day life.

I have discovered that when a person does free will, it triggers others to act from their mental imprint and do raging blame on the one doing free will. An understanding on all four of the power trips is that each one of them is a form of blaming rage and comes from this mental imprint inside each of us. You could say that even the slightest little trips are all coming from this mental imprint and are mild forms of rage. So really, if you start to do the system, i.e. free will, you will have to understand the 'story' of blaming rage since this opposition of others is exactly why people give up free will, as children, in the first place. That and they couldn't deal with their feelings.

Reiterating this problem of creation is to say that nearly **everyone acts from their mental imprint** against you when you 'do free will'. What does this mean to you the practitioner of the system? To answer this I must introduce another concept that will explain the essence of this situation.

In a very real sense **'it is all going on inside you'**. Outside reality is composed of persons, places and things. Inside reality is composed of the five energies that make up your being-ness. Since we have these imprints inside us, of fear and rage and grief, it is here that we need to work—not with other people. If you were able to heal these imprints inside you, the reflection other people would give you would be harmonious and they wouldn't want to rage at you any more.

Everyone in creation has their own reflection to give others. On earth, the major reflection most people give others is that of tribalism and power tripping and it will show up when you practice free will (the system). The main idea, on this, is that people are reflecting the imprint of the mental rage inside of you that is dead set against your own will being free.

Now, the juicy truth is that all people, from the two extremes—of a murderer rapist at one end to an independent freedom lover at the other end and every degree between these extremes—are true reflections of you. Because you have the imprint that says 'mind kill the will', inside you, the murderers and power trippers are reflecting this imprint to you. The point is that in a really big way 'it is all going on inside the individual.

Now—get this—by them raging at you when you do free will they are 'ringing' your mental imprint inside you and causing you to get onto your will's imprint of fear. In this fashion they are using your own energy against you. It is because we have these imprints inside each of us that **the opposition to free will is coming from inside the self and not primarily from others**—they just reflect what's going on inside you. Inside you are three pools of emotion—one pool of rage, one pool of fear and one pool of grief. Heal these emotions and your outer reflection will change.

This is all well and good and explains the 'mechanics' of the opposition you will encounter in the process of doing 'the system', but what to do about it? You can heal your imprints with the assistance of God's channeled books to Ceanne Derohan but until you do you will still have to learn good and evil and deal with the power tripper. Therefore, what exactly is the tribalist doing to the free will people?

Guilt, fear, pain, grief, and feeling his hatred of you for being independent, are what the tribalist wants you to feel when he attacks you. You can know that these five are all he can influence you to feel with his power trips—nothing more. If you understand and deal with each of these feelings he has no more power over you. So let's take them (again), one at a time and examine them.

If you have a problem with guilt and don't know if you are guilty on any issue or not, then, you need to understand right and wrong more thoroughly. Doing so is going to allow you to know true guilt (individual rights violations) from false guilt (violations against the tribe). When you embrace the knowledge of these two ethical systems and prove to yourself that independence is true and tribalism is false, you will be able to know that what the tribalist is doing is trying to make you feel false guilt. With this knowledge you will be able to not buy into his false guilt trips—I mean, you know better about right and wrong then the dumb tribalist. Good, their guilt trips are now not a problem for you.

Fear, the next one, is usually triggered in you by the tribalist raging at you. The other source of fear is seeing, when you do free will, others expressing 'hatred of the good for being good'. But what if you have felt fear, as I have recommended earlier in this book, and your capacity for feeling it includes feeling fear to the degree of shear terror? The tribalist, then, can get nowhere with his raging at you. The only caution you should be aware of is if his raging would turn into him doing violence to you in this rage state. Perhaps, as one defense, you could get out of the free will state when this occurs, until the danger passes.

Pain, the next one, is exactly what the fear trip threatens and this is why someone raging at you is so scary. Fear is telling you that one of your values is being threatened, namely, your body. This is the most potent reflection that could make you give up free will and this raging is one of the primary weapons the tribalist can use against you.

But, what if you were to start accepting pain in your process of accepting all of your other emotions? Doesn't it make sense, then, that your fear of a rager would cease to be such a scary thing? It is exactly his knowledge that you will do as he says because you don't want to accept the pain he will inflict on you if you don't. This is exactly the force behind the ethics of tribalism.

In my case, it has been the non-acceptance of the emotion of pain that fueled my paranoid fear inside me and when I began to understand that it was pain that I had to accept, most of my fear evaporated. Fine, how does one begin to accept pain so it is no big deal to feel it?

There are two types of pain: physical pain and emotional pain. These two have a lot in common and the acceptance of and the studying of them, when you feel them, is going to give you the knowledge of what they are and how they feel. Remember that the power of acceptance is another word for love and so, when you accept your pain you are loving it.

I play tennis every day for 1.3 hours and I have always had an aversion for physical effort throughout my past. It has been my **acceptance** for the physical pain that accompanies sports—my lungs screaming for oxygen and my muscles aching from me pushing my body to the limit—that has allowed me to know these pain feelings. Knowing and accepting pain is exactly what diminishes my fear since I know that pain is what fear threatens and **I know pain.**

Emotional pain can be understood and accepted in a similar manner and will cease to be something mysterious and unknown. This will allow you to soar ever higher in the realms of ecstasy brought to you by accepting your feelings and following the true ethics of independence and freedom.

Grief is going to come upon you as a response to learning that tribalism, the death philosophy is predominant in the world instead of free will. Remember to accept, feel and express your grief in order to heal your grief. By you accepting it and allowing it to express is exactly the actions that will heal it (the same for your fear and rage). However, don't get bogged down in it to where you stay in grief for days on end. Remember that free will is going to be established soon and this is a cheery note for your heart.

Feeling hated by the tribalist is yet another attempt to get you to give up free will. On this particular attack the tribalist has no foundation in hating you. It is just like him saying he hates goodness, life and anyone who practices it. Fine, he should just ignore you if he so hates it and leave you alone, but no, he has to try to cause you to give up free will by him hating you for it. When people express this hatred to me I see through them and know that they would never express it if they didn't think it might force me to give up free will. I feel contempt for them when they lay this hate trip on me and I usually say something back to them, telepathically, to let them know that they are dead wrong. Telepathy is a very useful tool.

*   *   *

Why the tribalist thinks you will give up reason and free will.

A curious thing about mister power tripper is that he cannot stand for anyone to do free will in his presence. What the hell does he care what others do? He does care—he simply can't stand for anyone to do free will. This implies that he is betting all his money on the power of the power trips as an ultimate force that he believes no one can resist. After all he gave into tribalism himself because he couldn't resist it when his significant others challenged him when he was doing free will as a child. If someone does resist his trips he comes 'unglued'. Of course, this position he takes is indicative as to how he views others, or more specifically how he thinks others should be, namely, no one should do free will. His view of others is not as independent equals like it should be, it is something else. He somehow believes that he must have 'a say' in the behavior of the others around him instead of him respecting their self soveirgnty. This indicates that his viewpoint of others is tribalistic in nature.

With this tribal view what the tribalist is doing is trying to force the tribalist ethics down the throat of all people who strive to gain free will. He watches others like a hawk watches its prey and when the free will practitioner acts in a way that violates the tribalist's ethics, namely, being free, he power trips him to make him bend to his idea of right and wrong. Since his ethics are the false ethics of tribalism he is the one who is wrong. But, what is really going on is he is rationalizing the power trips in order to think it's moral to power trip so he can psychologically kill the feelings of the free will people around him and, simultaneously, believe he is doing something else, namely, enforcing what is good and right in the name of tribalism. To this end he has convinced himself that tribalism is true. Why, because it is the system that kills free will and it is the will he wants to keep down—in himself and in others. The reason he wants to kill the will is because if he didn't he would have to deal with the emotions.

I often wondered why most people are moralists; I now know that it is expressly being a moralist, complete with the accompanying power trips, that kills the will, i.e. if they didn't want to keep the will down in themselves and in others they would never be so consumed on being such fanatics for the morals of tribalism. By the way, God is saying the same thing when he said 'they are worshipping guilt instead of worshipping him'. (This comes from his channeled books to Ceanne DeRohan.) The question then comes down to how to deal with a world full of will killers? As surely as you draw breath, when you do free will and feel wonderful about it, the masses will assault you with their 'power trips'.

The truth of the power tripper is he holds the evil morals of tribalism and he power trips the free person in the name of tribalism. In order to maintain this stand **he lies to himself** and says: 1. Tribalism is the true ethics and 2. Power tripping is good. It is these two lies that allow him to attack the free will state. Without these two lies his opposition to the free will ethics wouldn't work. In conclusion, then, **he is a power tripper and a liar**. These are the two distinguishing characteristics of his psychology.

OK, fine, he is affronting reality with his lies and he is guilty—in the truth—of violating the rights of others in the name of tribalism. Surely there must be something the free will advocates, who live in the truth, can use that would defend free will against such contemptible lying power trippers. Sort of hold the tribalist to the truth, as it were. I mean the tribalist is riddled with true guilt and lies to himself, so you would think that it would be easy to defeat such an abberated person.

The basic fact is that when a person does free will in the presence of others he will meet, ultimately, murderous blaming rage from the people around him. Anyone practicing free will triggers the gap where this murderous hatred exits. In the light of this it is no wonder that civilization had a really hard time trying to establish independence—individual rights. It still isn't established because no one realizes what is creating the opposition to this.

The ultimate reason for the establishment of tribalism lies within the self. Denying the will inside the individual led to the establishment of tribalism as a cultural morality.

The solution then doesn't lie with other people it lays within each individual and it is denial of the will that must be replaced with the acceptance of free will and the ethics of individualism.

OK, when you do free will you get the reflection of a force that is against this. Fine, that opposition is coming from within you and is actually the imprints of the mind wanting to have power over the will—the feelings—this is the exact reflection that is going on in outer reality, namely that others cannot allow you to do free will. This means that the imprints inside each of us 'have it' that the mind is the ruler and the will has to serve the mind and thus tribalism rules—instead of the will being an equal with the mind and that each is not to dominate the other and that individual rights rule. What this means is that everyone has his/her mind in the power position and their poor will has to serve instead of being regarded as a soveirgn equal. This imbalance of these two energies is exactly what following the tribal ethics results in and it has always been the denial of the will that has been the main issue at the heart of the tribalist ethics. This is indicative of the type of evolution we have, namely, 'denial of the will' evolving into 'acceptance of the will'. In ethical terms we are seeing the falseness of tribalism and the truth of independence.

The imprint of the mental level inside each of us is composed of immense rage against the emotions; the imprint of the emotional level is composed of immense fear of the mental level's rage. This plays out with people when the tribalist starts raging at the free will person for doing free will and tries to drive him onto his will's fear imprint. The rager hopes to gain power over the free will advocate in this manner and the reason he thinks he will obey him is because if he doesn't he will do a fear trip on him by threatening murder. He thinks that you do not want to feel fear and so you will do as he says to prevent him from making you feel fear.

In ethical terms, tribalism rules because it is the system in accordance with the imprints of 'mind dominates the will' and 'don't let the will be free'. But the truth we are all evolving into is going to topple this tyranny by recognizing that **'feel equals think' and that 'the will has to be free'**. Of course it is mainly fear, pain and guilt that no one knows how to deal with that causes people to think tribalism is true.

Never the less to heal yourself entails achieving a workable relationship with people, such that you aren't being power tripped and therefore your relations are not damaging to you. Being psychologically independent is going to facilitate success with your relations with others. This out of the way, you can focus on your self; learning to accept your will and healing it; learning how to function in non-denial etc. etc. In the next chapter I will be focusing exactly on the self in relation to itself.

CHAPTER FIVE

How to live in happiness!

What the whole human experience boils down to is most people buy into the tribalist ethics for one reason and one reason only—because they do not know how to deal with their feelings. Tribalism effectively shuts them down and that is why people buy into it. When you follow individual rights you will have to deal with your feelings, there is no way around it. This appears as such a huge task because three of the emotions, namely, fear, pain and guilt, are difficult to deal with.

I can sympathize with the tribalists because to accept the emotions is so big that I can actually say that I don't blame anyone for embracing tribalism. However, if I were to show you how to manage the emotions in a way that will allow you to live in the truth of free will and not get blown away by them, I believe I would be showing 'the way' for you to gain your happiness. No longer would you be plagued by uncertainty, confusion and hopeless sadness that results from following tribalism and not knowing your self.

Remember also that your mind, when it believed in tribalism, was endorsing contradictions since tribalism is the false ethics. So, when you embrace the true ethics of individualism your mind is now in the truth and will function in a more effective manner. With your mind thus freed up from contradictions it becomes more powerful and is a strong ally to have in balancing with your feelings in free will and individualism's truth, which I will illustrate shortly. With the knowledge of how to be, which is my next topic, I will put the feelings in the proper perspective that is going to allow for their management and healing.

*   *   *

How to be

So, the goal of life is to 'be'; but what does it mean to 'be'? Man is composed of five energies—mind, will, heart, body and conscious/subconscious (c/sc)—he thinks, feels, loves and sees. To 'be', means these energies are in their 'on' state. (Following tribalism gave each of us the experience of the 'off' state of these energies.) The symbol of the new age is '1111' and this refers to these first four energies in their 'on' state. The fifth energy is the c/sc, the attention point, the activator and maintainer of this balance. So then, what does it mean to have these four energies 'on'?

For your mind, it's 'on' when it 'knows' what your-self is doing (all five energies) and knows what is going on in the immediate surroundings. Of course, the mind can know the entirety of reality with its ability of thought but what I'm telling you here is that knowing what the self and its immediate environment is doing, is the ability of the mind that is most fundamental to achieving and maintaining the 'up' state of being. Then, when your mind is conscious of your other three energies, this influences these others to get into their up state also. On this, the mind is the leader of the other energies, i.e. start by getting your mind online then you can use it and your c/sc to get the others up.

With your mind on and focused on the self it knows the state of the feelings, i.e. what the feelings—the will—are feeling. The mind sort of knows and listens to the will and balances with it with full knowledge that the will is its 'equal' but that it, the will, focuses on the feel of things rather than the knowing of things like the mind. In this way the knowing and feeling balances with each other in the heart.

Your heart's main function is acceptance (love). This energy comes alive when it is accepting. The main thing it has to accept is the self. The mind can know what the heart is doing from moment to moment, e.g. whether it is in self acceptance or not.

Your fourth energy—the body—comes alive when it is seeing the beauty of the environment and/or listening to the 'music' of sound. Your c/sc or 'attention' can travel throughout all four energies and can be used to maintain these four in their on state.

So, consequently, when you are living with all four of these energies in their 'on' state, **'you are being'—'you are'—'and life is a lot of fun'.** You know, you feel, you love and you see; that is what you are and when these four are energized that is enough for you to live in complete satisfaction......life achieved!

What I am talking about is introspection; ask yourself, 'what are my four energies doing right here and right now'. There is much more to say about this living 1111 but the knowledge here should be enough to get you started in achieving this four way balance.

Now, to get back to dealing with your will in light of this balanced state of being. Realize that your will is exactly one fourth of being. What you want to do is to prevent the emotional expression from getting out of hand and causing you to get swept away in emotions. You can manage your will by getting your mind online and establishing order and harmony with all four energies. This doesn't mean that you deny feelings, you allow them to express but you prevent them from taking over the rest of your being.

The main point I want to make is that it is a very different thing to deal with the emotions when you are living in this online state then it is when your energies are down or offline. I used to stay in fear and guilt during a lot of time before I learned this up state of my energies. After I began practicing balance, my energies fell into their respective roles and I began to experience happiness.

It is really simple to turn your energies on and thus you will, while they are on, be happy. When you are not doing this 4 way balance you are less than happy; when you do this 4 way balance you are necessarily happy. Maintain this 'up' state balance and you will live in happiness! Be sure you don't earn true guilt by power tripping others and you are good to go.

This path I have been showing you throughout this book first explained what is going on with the masses of people—tribalism is the major morality. Then I explained why it is so—will denial and ignorance. Then, I showed you the many aspects of good and evil and thus offered a way to live in this knowledge in a guiltless fashion. This knowledge answered a lot of questions about the moral aspect of human behavior so that knowingness could be gained of what you and other people are doing. This, then, opened the door for you to focus on your being primarily and learn what it is. This led to learning how happiness can be obtained by you—balancing your four energies in their up state.

The only thing left that I want to say in this book is to list 'little tricks' that will help you bring your being up to the knowing and living of these ideas.

*   *   *

Tricks of the trade (of living)

Trick number one: In denying your mind you may get washed away by fear, pain and guilt. I learned, through introspection, that when I deny my mind these three emotions take me over. In this anti-mind state I am at the mercy of any chance influence around me and I see the world as a guilty person would, and in fear of everything. When I turn my mind on, all of that disappears. Therefore, balance of my energies is the solution.

Trick number two: If you are washed away by your emotions you can gain some kind of balance from the art of turning your mind on and thereby sharing your attention between your mind and your feelings. To do this give your mind a task. For example ask yourself to describe the surroundings that your eyes see, in the most logical and succinct words you can, focusing on the words, primarily. Alternatively ask your mind to describe what your feelings are right here and right now. By learning to put into words what your energies are seeing, feeling and accepting, you are exercising your knowing in its wonderful job of introspection. After all it is the minds job to be the great 'knower', just as it is the job of the will to be the great feeler and the job of the heart to be the great acceptor and the body's job to be the great seer. Finally it is the job of the c/sc to be the great maintainer of the balance of these first four energies.

Trick number three: I can only tell you what works for me in dealing with the people around me. First, if you are minding your own business by keeping your consciousness centered on what you are doing and you are ignoring the others around you, it can eliminate a lot of problems with others. While doing this you must not power trip others neither in thought nor deed. God's advice on this subject is: "power tripping in any direction is not right use of will". Not power tripping is so wonderful and so right that it feels the best and you can be sure you are being socially moral in the most perfect way.

However, when some people notice me and start to power trip me I sometimes respond by power tripping him/her back. I mean the person is being dead wrong in trying to overpower me with his 'trips' and I am in the 'right'—I am just trying to live my life in the joy of free will. I usually power trip him/her back with using telepathy and I rage at him and tell him what a worthless piece of xxxx he is for power tripping me which is actually a true guilt trip I'm laying on him. But—and here is the point—if you keep your consciousness focused on your self and ignore the other but recognize that he is acting immoral and at the same time don't buy into what his power trip is trying to cause you to feel, you can 'stop him cold' since his power trip failed to get a response from you.

How you can do this is by asserting to yourself that you listen only to yourself and not to others. You know that you are sometimes going to get power tripped but since you are convinced that your relationship you have with yourself is primary and all others take second place to this you can allow yourself to never buy into any of the trips people throw at you. I mean you are going to listen to yourself and not others. Of course, if the power tripper is threatening violence be wary of him/her and take measures to de-fuse the situation.

I found out, further, that a great way to deal with the outside world is to not do free will in the presence of others and, therefore, I wouldn't trigger their opposition. To add to this I realized that since the work I need to do involves me with my self only, I discovered, yet another secret: when I focus my attention on my self and ignore others this frees them up from my interference and shows them that focus on the self is the most proper way to be. When you maintain this state of self focus you become independent from others and if they try to power trip you it has little effect. Because you know that others are of secondary concern you can discount their importance to you and because you know what and why they power trip, in the first place, you can not buy into any adverse effect they may want to hook you into to with their power trips.

Trick number four: Introspection, or watching yourself, is an art that you will have to develop if you want to balance in the up state of self. I have developed this habit of watching myself and when I feel something, for example, I am aware that I am feeling and usually why I'm feeling it. I ask 'what am I doing', to guide my 'understanding' in looking at my centers and put into words what I am doing in each present moment.

A very useful concept you can use in this process of introspection is to remember the goals of the four centers. Thus, you want your mind in mental focus. This presupposes you learn when your mind is aligned with reason's truth and when it is operating from misjudgments. The first state is the mind's up state and the second state is mind's down state. Next, the will has an up state and a down state; emotions alive equals the up state; emotions denied (not feeling anything) equals its down state. The heart's up state is accepting the self and its down state is non acceptance of the self. The body's up state is seeing the truth of beauty of the physical world and its down state is seeing the world but it doesn't look beautiful.

Trick number five: As the conditions in your life change, like a kaleidoscope, you will see that it is sometimes appropriate to focus more intently in one or the other of the four energies. Sometimes, it is appropriate to think. Sometimes it is appropriate to feel….. or accept…. or see…. So the correct way to be has two parts: 1-maintaining a 'quiescent' state of balance of all four energies—all 'up', and 2-focusing in one or another center as appropriate.

By maintaining a quiescent state of awareness of these four energies you are in a balanced state that doesn't deny any of the four energies. In a manner, you have your fifth energy (C/SC), being aware of all four other energies equally and you can shift your attention to one or another, easily, as necessary. This quiescent state is the state you can 'always come back to'. For example, you are studying a schoolbook and you are focused in your mental center. You then take a break and you come back to this quiescent state where all four of your energies are in a position of equality. Likewise, you may need to focus more on your body energy by going into what your eyes are seeing. For example, you see a girl that is drop dead gorgeous, you then focus on what you see to the exclusion of the other three energies. After you have seen enough, you again comeback to the quiescent state.

Trick number six: If you remember that we needed the experience of power tripping in order to understand evil, (look back at the history of civilization that we all had reincarnational lives in), and that that experience is coming to an end, we all can now learn the glorious and wonderful truth that each of us can 'go for it for ourselves' provided we respect others right to do the same. In other words, the human race is about to graduate from the school of hard knocks of tribalism. Thus, we can herald in the Age of Aquarius—the age of Free Will!

Trick number seven: Sure, in my experience I still run into scenarios where a person or persons want to power trip me but when they do I call to mind that "I live unto myself" and I don't care what others do. Because I maintain independence, I am not buying into their trips so they don't affect me. Concurrently, I refrain from power tripping them back and focus my consciousness away from them and, more times than not, this is enough for them to stop with their power trips. I mean, they can get nowhere with me, so they give up and leave me alone.

Trick number eight: The truth is that, OK, the imprints are inside each of us but, what the tribalist has to overcome first in you, in order to stop you doing free will, is your **independent state of being.** Unless he first kills your independence of him he can get no where with you. It's here that you can hold out against the tribalist by not giving up your independence. He will give up on his power trips because he can't push your buttons anymore.

Trick number nine: We all need God's light to live so ask him to fill you with light—often. He has said that he is open to communicate with each and every one of us so the door is finally open to talk to him one on one.

Trick number ten: Stay independent, work on yourself, and realize the main purpose of your relations with others is to celebrate life as independent beings. Remember that the only way to experience the oneness of creation is to achieve and maintain independence.

CHEERS!

GLOSSARY

Aesthetics: the branch of philosophy that describes the role of Art as a fuel source by showing values in a perceptual form so the viewer can perceive them directly. Ex., a movie that depicts the hero overcoming great obstacles and getting the girl in the end. Here the viewer can see someone achieving values and he feels fueled up to continue to pursue his own values and life.

Body/sight energy: the fourth part of being, either God or each of us; this energy is responsible for creating form and its major characteristic is its visual faculty.

Conscious/subconscious energy: this is the fifth part of being either God or each of us; it's called the orchestrator energy and its job is to coordinate the actions of the other four energies.

Death philosophy: the system of tribalism where the individual is subjugated to the tribe and has no moral significance other than serving the welfare of the tribe; self sacrifice is seen to be the highest good.

Discernment: this is the process of correctly identifying the facts of reality and obeys all the rules of reason; as opposed to judging reality which is a misapprehension of the facts of reality. We should learn to discriminate when we are discerning—or 'judging' the facts.

Emotion: the feeling energy's expression of value appraisals: fear, pain, guilt, rage, hate, grief and joy are the predominant emotions and gives a running tally of how the being is doing moment by moment in terms of values being frustrated or achieved.

Epistemology: the branch of philosophy that studies the process of knowing and the nature of knowledge.

Ethics: the branch of philosophy that studies the nature of right and wrong.

Evil: (social) those actions that violate the rights of the individual in favor of the false ethics of tribalism, the death philosophy.

Evolution: the progression of civilization to come from the default philosophy of tribalism into the true philosophy of free will/independence.

Fear: the emotion that is mostly denied in evolution and because tribalism denies free will, eliminates having to deal with the fear. The true philosophy of free will accepts fear and promotes expression as a means of healing it—realizing that to not accept it keeps it in denial which is an unhealthy practice for the being.

Fear trip: One of the tribalist's weapons against those who practice free will to try to instill fear in order to make him give up free will.

Free will: In the ethics of independence free will is where the will (feeling body) is recognized as necessary to the well being of the being and needs to be free. Unlike the ethics of tribalism that upholds denying free will completely.

Good: the well being of the individual in practicing the ethics of free will/reason and where no interference of other peoples lives takes place.

Guilt: 2 varieties: true guilt is where the individual rights of a person are violated usually with the power trips, theft and murder. False guilt is violating the ethics of tribalism. Since tribalism is the false ethics abhorrent to independence, violating them consists of false guilt because they don't violate the true ethics of independence. The tribalist, however, believes otherwise—but then he is suffering under the illusions of tribalism.

Guilt trip: One of the tribalist's weapons against those who practice free will to try to instill guilt in order to make him give up free will.

Hate: something strongly disliked—the opposite of love/ acceptance—a form of not accepting—rejection.

Hate trip: one of the tribalist's weapons against those who practice free will that tries to make the free one give it up because the tribalist hates him for it.

Heart/love energy: The third energy of being and is responsible for 'accepting' reality and is where the spirit and will energies balance.

Hierarchy: of thoughts is where some thoughts being more inclusive and more general are in a higher position than derivative or more specific thoughts. Ex. 'Thing' is a very general word and includes many, many other words—conversely the word lamp is a 'thing' but it describes a narrower category so it is below the word 'thing' hierarchically.

Independence: self sufficient, morally and psychologically. Able to live free and unencumbered without detrimental psychological ties to any other being.

Independent equals: the way all people should be regarded; one shouldn't look up to or down at another but to treat them as equals.

Individual rights: those rights that each person possesses, namely, to live ones life in a manner as the individual see's fit providing it does not infringe on those same rights of others.

Inner Reality: the reality of the individual with the relationships of the five energies that compose his being—not in relation to outer reality, e.g. the mind in relation with the will etc. etc.

Joy: happiness—the result of practicing moral perfection.

Judgments: contradictory statements held as true. These normally have a kernel of truth but are laced with contradictions. To master the art of non contradictory thinking is a must for ones spirit/mental energy's evolution.

Lost will: that portion of the feelings that are heavily denied and are held down in the subconscious. Rage fear and grief compose a big part of it.

Love: acceptance is another word for love. To lovingly accept all of reality especially the self is the divine plan for all.

Metaphysics: The name of the first branch of philosophy that tells the basic nature of being and reality.

Net of tribalism: composed of all those people who practice the false ethics of tribalism and are actively against anyone who practice the true ethics of free will/independence.

Order trip: one of the four trips tribalists use against the free will practitioners. Telling someone what to do implies the power tripper knows better than his victim as to how to lead his life. This is an attempt to become a 'significant other' to the independent person, and is immoral.

Outer Reality: the material universe—physical reality—composed of space, energy, time and matter.

Pain: emotional pain can be the response to someone violating your rights.

Perfect: morally perfect is when you practice the ethics of independence—never violating others rights.

Philosophy: The body of knowledge that deals with the most important issues in regards to the nature of man and the universe; how to know it; and good and evil.

Politics: the branch of philosophy that deals with societies and nations and how they should behave—derived from ethics.

Power trips: orders, guilt trips, fear trips and hate trips are the most common way the tribalists use to psychologically kill the free will person.

Rage: an emotion that is a big part of lost will and heavily judged against. To express it alone and by yourself in the name of expressing how you feel and not to make it a habit is the healing action it needs.

Reason: the art and science of non-contradictory thinking—discerning reality instead of falsely identifying it via judgments.

Self Esteem: the opposite emotion of guilt—to achieve moral perfection will result in a constant state of self esteem—feeling 'right for reality'—as you grow you will get to know this emotion and it feels really good.

Spirit/mental energy: the living energy that deals with thoughts and is one part of being-ness.

Tribalism: the opposite ethics to free will/independence. The tribe is considered all and the individual an inconsequential part that must sacrifice for others—the death philosophy.

Truth structure: the thought structure each person possesses and is composed of those thoughts the person holds as the truth of reality—the thoughts can be true discernments or judgments in any part of it.

Value: right and wrong are a subdivision of this concept—emotions express the person's values, i.e. what the person regards as important and valuable—worthy of effort to gain and achieve.

Value structure: each person possesses one; the emotions a person expresses in response to reality show what values reside in this value structure.

Will/feeling energy: the living energy that deals with feelings (sensations) and is one part of being-ness.